Documents of American Democracy

BILL OF RIGHTS

Katie Kawa

PowerKiDS press.

New York

Published in 2017 by The Rosen Publishing Group, Inc.
29 East 21st Street, New York, NY 10010

Editor: Katie Kawa
Book Design: Tanya Dellaccio

Photo Credits: Cover (painting) Courtesy of the Library of Congress; Cover (document) https://commons.wikimedia.org/wiki/File:Bill_of_Rights_Pg1of1_AC.jpg; Background (all pages except 27) didecs/Shutterstock.com; p. 5 Alex Wong/Getty Images; p. 6 https://commons.wikimedia.org/wiki/File:The_Federalist_(1st_ed,_1788,_vol_I,_title_page)_-_02.jpg; p. 7 https://commons.wikimedia.org/wiki/File:Scene_at_the_Signing_of_the_Constitution_of_the_United_States.jpg; p. 9 https://commons.wikimedia.org/wiki/File:James_Madison.jpg; p. 11 Courtesy of the National Archives; p. 13 lev radin/Shutterstock.com; p. 15 (top) Creativa Images/Shutterstock.com; p. 15 (bottom) Andrey_Popov/Shutterstock.com; p. 17 Rolls Press/Popperfoto/Getty Images; p. 19 Hulton Archive/Getty Images; p. 21 David Kocherhans/Shutterstock.com; p. 23 Ron Chapple/Getty Images; p. 25 corgarashu/Shutterstock.com; p. 27 (document) Aaron Haupt/Getty Images; p. 27 (background) James Whelan/Shutterstock.com.

Library of Congress Cataloging-in-Publication Data

Names: Kawa, Katie, author.
Title: Bill of Rights / Katie Kawa.
Description: New York : PowerKids Press, 2016. | Series: Documents of American democracy | Includes index.
Identifiers: LCCN 2016005030 | ISBN 9781499420739 (pbk.) | ISBN 9781499420753 (library bound) | ISBN 9781499420746 (6 pack)
Subjects: LCSH: United States. Constitution. 1st-10th Amendments–Juvenile literature. | Civil rights–United States–Juvenile literature.
Classification: LCC KF4749 .K39 2016 | DDC 342.7308/5–dc23
LC record available at http://lccn.loc.gov/2016005030

Manufactured in the United States of America

CPSIA Compliance Information: Batch #BS16PK: For Further Information contact Rosen Publishing, New York, New York at 1-800-237-9932

CONTENTS

PROTECTING INDIVIDUAL RIGHTS

The protection of individual rights has been an important part of American democracy since the nation's earliest days. The Declaration of Independence states all men have the right to "Life, Liberty and the pursuit of Happiness." Once the United States had its own Constitution, the question of how the government could best protect those individual rights arose. This led to the creation of the first 10 amendments, or changes, to the U.S. Constitution, which are commonly known as the Bill of Rights.

The Bill of Rights is known today as one of the most important documents in U.S. history. These amendments were ratified, or approved, on December 15, 1791. More than 200 years later, they still influence the lives of the American people and the actions of the government that serves them.

Visitors to Washington, D.C., can view one of the original copies of the Bill of Rights at the National Archives, shown here.

FEDERALISTS AND ANTI-FEDERALISTS

The Bill of Rights was created because of debates surrounding the U.S. Constitution. The Constitution wasn't immediately accepted after it was written. It needed to be ratified by the states first.

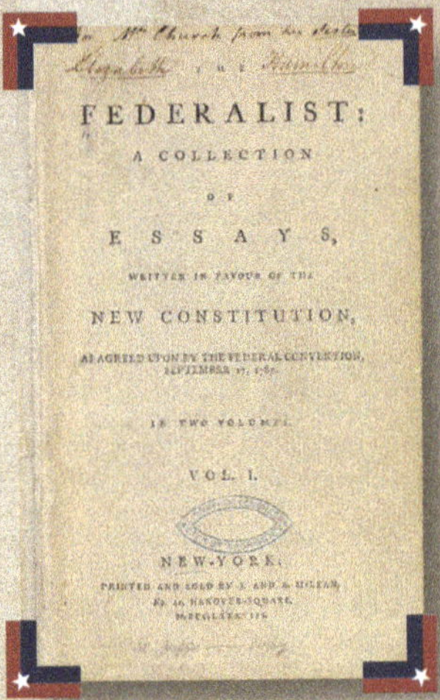

During this ratification process, U.S. leaders were divided into two main groups: Federalists, who supported the Constitution, and Anti-Federalists, who didn't support the document

THE FEDERALIST PAPERS

While the Anti-Federalists called for a bill of rights among other changes to the Constitution, the Federalists tried to create support for the Constitution. One way they did this was through a series of 85 essays published as The Federalist. *Today, they're more commonly known as the Federalist Papers. These essays were written by Alexander Hamilton, James Madison, and John Jay. They argued that the Constitution wouldn't take away individual rights and would help create a more stable government for America.*

as it had been written. One of the Anti-Federalists' main complaints was that the Constitution could allow the federal government to become too powerful. They worried that states' rights and individual rights could be taken away. This fear led many to call for a bill of rights to be added to the new Constitution. In fact, certain states, such as North Carolina, didn't ratify the Constitution until they knew it would contain a bill of rights.

After fighting for independence from Britain, many Americans feared giving the federal government too much power. They worried their individual rights were at risk. This was at the heart of many debates between Federalists and Anti-Federalists.

MADISON LEARNS FROM MASON

It soon became clear—even to many Federalists—that a bill of rights needed to be added to the Constitution in order for Americans to believe their rights were protected. James Madison became an influential supporter of the inclusion of a bill of rights. As a congressman, he went through the possible amendments suggested by the states and used them to create what would become the Bill of Rights.

Madison was inspired by different historical documents as he put together the Bill of Rights. One of these documents was the Virginia Declaration of Rights, which was written in 1776 by George Mason. This declaration allowed for freedom of the press and religious freedom, which are two important parts of the Bill of Rights. The Virginia Declaration of Rights also inspired Thomas Jefferson as he wrote the Declaration of Independence.

In a letter to Thomas Jefferson written in 1788, James Madison stated, "My own opinion has always been in favor of a bill of rights."

JAMES MADISON

APPROVING THE AMENDMENTS

On June 8, 1789, Madison officially proposed his set of amendments to the U.S. Constitution during a meeting of Congress. At first, Madison wanted to change the words of the Constitution itself. However, it was later decided that the Bill of Rights should be added as a separate part of the Constitution.

The U.S. House of Representatives approved 17 amendments proposed by Madison. The Senate then approved 12. Finally, on September 25, 1789, those 12 amendments were proposed to state legislatures.

FROM 12 TO 10

What happened to the other two amendments proposed to the states? One was never ratified by enough states. It dealt with the number of members of the House of Representatives and how that should relate to the population. The other rejected amendment concerned changing the amount of money members of Congress were paid. It finally became the 27th Amendment on May 7, 1992. These two amendments are still included on the original copy of the Bill of Rights on display at the National Archives.

Shown here is New York State's official declaration that it ratified 11 of the 12 amendments proposed by Congress. Each amendment needed to have the support of three-fourths of the state legislatures. This is why not every amendment proposed became part of the Bill of Rights.

In order for the Bill of Rights to be adopted, it needed to be ratified by three-fourths of the state legislatures. This happened on December 15, 1791, thanks to the Virginia state legislature. Three-fourths of the state legislatures ratified 10 of the 12 amendments. Those 10 amendments are the Bill of Rights as we know it today.

THE FIRST AMENDMENT AND RELIGION

The First Amendment to the U.S. Constitution outlines several basic rights the U.S. government can't deny its citizens. It protects freedom of religion, freedom of speech, freedom of the press, the right to assemble peacefully, and the right to **petition** the government.

Freedom of religion continues to be an important part of the Bill of Rights. The First Amendment states that Americans can practice their chosen religion freely, without fear of **persecution** by the federal government. Not every country protects religious freedom. In fact, people have been coming to America to escape religious persecution since colonial times.

Today, the United States is a country made up of people with a wide variety of religious beliefs. Thanks to the First Amendment, Americans can express these beliefs openly.

ARTICLE THE THIRD

"Congress shall make no law respecting an establishment of religion, or prohibiting the free exercise thereof; or abridging the freedom of speech, or of the press; or the right of the people peaceably to assemble, and to petition the Government for a redress of grievances."

*What we now call the First Amendment is actually the Third Amendment—or "Article the third"—according to the original copy of the proposed Bill of Rights. This amendment has allowed for the religious **diversity** seen across America today.*

FREE SPEECH

The First Amendment to the U.S. Constitution also protects people's right to say and write things without being punished by the federal government. This includes things that are critical of the government and statements that might be thought of as offensive or unkind. Freedom of the press protects people who write for and own newspapers, websites, TV news channels, and other professional media outlets. The press isn't granted more freedom than ordinary citizens when it comes to what they say and write.

This part of the First Amendment is meant to be considered with care. While many kinds of speech are protected under this amendment, some words can still be hurtful to other people. Also, the press isn't free to publish lies and claim they're the truth.

Freedom of speech and freedom of the press are important parts of a free country. They're just as important today as they were when the Bill of Rights was created.

ASSEMBLY AND PETITION

The final two rights guaranteed under the First Amendment are the right to assemble peaceably, or peacefully, and the right to petition the government. The federal government can't keep people from gathering together or forming groups, as long as they're doing it in a peaceful way. This includes political parties, community groups, and religious organizations.

The First Amendment protects a U.S. citizen's right to ask government officials for things they think the government should do. It also protects their right to ask the government to make changes. Both of these actions are ways to petition the government, which is a First Amendment right. Because of this amendment, lobbyists can do their job. A lobbyist is a person paid to try to get a lawmaker to support a certain business or cause.

The First Amendment grants U.S. citizens the right to peacefully assemble to protest. During the civil rights movement that reached its peak in the 1960s, many Americans exercised this right. People continue to exercise this right through peaceful protests today.

KEEPING THE PEACE

When considering the right to assemble, the most important word is "peaceably." The federal government can take action if a group isn't meeting in a peaceful way. For example, a group could gather to protest a law they feel is unjust. As long as they're protesting peacefully, that's within the rights granted to them through the First Amendment. However, if their protest turns into a violent ***riot****, the federal government can take action to break it up.*

THE RIGHT TO BEAR ARMS

The Second Amendment to the U.S. Constitution protects U.S. citizens' right to "keep and bear Arms." This means U.S. citizens are allowed to own weapons, such as guns, knives, and swords, without interference from the federal government. At the time the Bill of Rights was written, this amendment was put in place in order for each state to have a strong militia. A militia is a group of citizens that can serve as a military force if needed.

The Second Amendment is the subject of many debates in the United States today. Is it within ordinary citizens' rights to own weapons that were originally made for military use? Do gun control laws interfere with Americans' Second Amendment rights? These are questions U.S. leaders are still trying to answer.

The Second Amendment was ***drafted*** *to ensure that each state had a strong militia in case the states needed to defend themselves against a federal government that abused its power. During the American Revolution, shown here, battles were fought by militias.*

RIGHTS AND RESPONSIBILITIES

*An important part of citizenship is understanding there are responsibilities that go along with your rights. The Second Amendment protects U.S. citizens' right to own weapons, but they're expected to act responsibly when it comes to owning and using these weapons. There are many laws in place that govern the use of weapons in order to **ensure** the safety of all Americans. If a person chooses not to follow these laws, they might be fined or even sent to jail.*

ARTICLE THE FOURTH

"A well regulated Militia, being necessary to the security of a free State, the right of the people to keep and bear Arms, shall not be infringed."

PROTECTING PRIVATE PROPERTY

Protection of private property has always been very important to Americans, and that's reflected in the Bill of Rights. The Third Amendment states that Americans don't have to quarter, or keep, soldiers in their homes.

The Fourth Amendment begins a section of the Bill of Rights focused on the rights of someone accused of committing a crime. This amendment protects Americans from "unreasonable searches and seizures." This means a law enforcement authority—or any other person—can't search a person's private property, home, or body unless they have a detailed **warrant**. They also can't seize, or take, anything from a person without a warrant. In order to search or seize property, the warrant has to show that the law enforcement official has a good reason to do so.

Because of the Fourth Amendment, police officers must have a warrant before searching a home or another piece of private property.

QUARTERING TROOPS

Why was the fear of being forced to quarter troops so strong in the United States after the American Revolution? Before the war, Britain kept soldiers in its American colonies. They stayed in the private homes of colonists, and the colonists had no say in the matter. This also happened during the war. Americans wanted to know this wouldn't happen in their new nation, which is why the Third Amendment was included in the Bill of Rights.

ARTICLE THE SIXTH

"The right of the people to be secure in their persons, houses, papers, and effects, against unreasonable searches and seizures, shall not be violated, and no Warrants shall issue, but upon probable cause, supported by Oath or affirmation, and particularly describing the place to be searched, and the persons or things to be seized."

PLEADING THE FIFTH

Protection of private property is also part of the Fifth Amendment. It states that the U.S. government must pay a person if the government takes over their property.

The Fifth Amendment also states that a grand jury must decide if a person accused of a serious crime—especially a crime punishable by death—should be put on trial. This amendment protects against a person being put on trial twice for the same crime, which is called double jeopardy. In addition, it protects people from being witnesses against themselves in court.

Finally, the Fifth Amendment ensures that a person can't be fined, jailed, or sentenced to death for a crime "without due process of law." This means certain legal **procedures** must be followed before a person is punished for a crime.

ARTICLE THE SEVENTH

"No person shall be held to answer for a capital, or otherwise infamous crime, unless on a presentment or indictment of a Grand Jury, except in cases arising in the land or naval forces, or in the Militia, when in actual service in time of War or public danger; nor shall any person be subject for the same offence to be twice put in jeopardy of life or limb; nor shall be compelled in any criminal case to be a witness against himself, nor be deprived of life, liberty, or property, without due process of law; nor shall private property be taken for public use, without just compensation."

If a person feels something they might say in court will ***incriminate*** *them, they can exercise their Fifth Amendment rights. This is why it's sometimes said that a person "pleads the Fifth" while in court.*

RIGHTS IN THE COURTROOM

Not every country in the world ensures the right to a trial by jury, but it's an important part of the U.S. legal system. The Sixth Amendment grants Americans this right, as well as the right to a lawyer if they're accused of a crime. This amendment also protects "the right to a speedy and public trial."

The Seventh Amendment ensures that civil cases are tried by a jury if the property involved is worth more than $20. A civil case is a noncriminal lawsuit.

U.S. citizens are protected against "cruel and unusual punishments" through the Eighth Amendment. According to this amendment, people shouldn't have to pay "excessive" fines or bail if they're accused of a crime. Bail is money paid to free a person from jail until their trial.

The Eighth Amendment to the U.S. Constitution states, "Excessive bail shall not be required, nor excessive fines imposed, nor cruel and unusual punishments inflicted." This is worded almost exactly the same as part of the English Bill of Rights, which was written in 1689: "Excessive bail ought not to be required, nor excessive fines imposed, nor cruel and unusual punishments inflicted."

ADDITIONAL RIGHTS

The final two amendments that make up the Bill of Rights deal with rights and powers that aren't defined in the U.S. Constitution. The Ninth Amendment makes it clear that the rights expressed in this document aren't the only rights Americans have. These additional rights exist and shouldn't be taken away just because they're not written in the Constitution or the Bill of Rights.

The 10th Amendment gives the states and the citizens of those states any powers not specifically granted to the federal government in the Constitution.

These two amendments reflect the main reason why the Bill of Rights was created. They help limit the power of the federal government and protect all individual rights.

The Bill of Rights continues to be the center of discussions and debates about Americans' individual rights. It's important to know these 10 amendments in order to understand some of your basic rights as an American citizen.

"Article" means part of a document.

New York City was the capital of the United States in 1789.

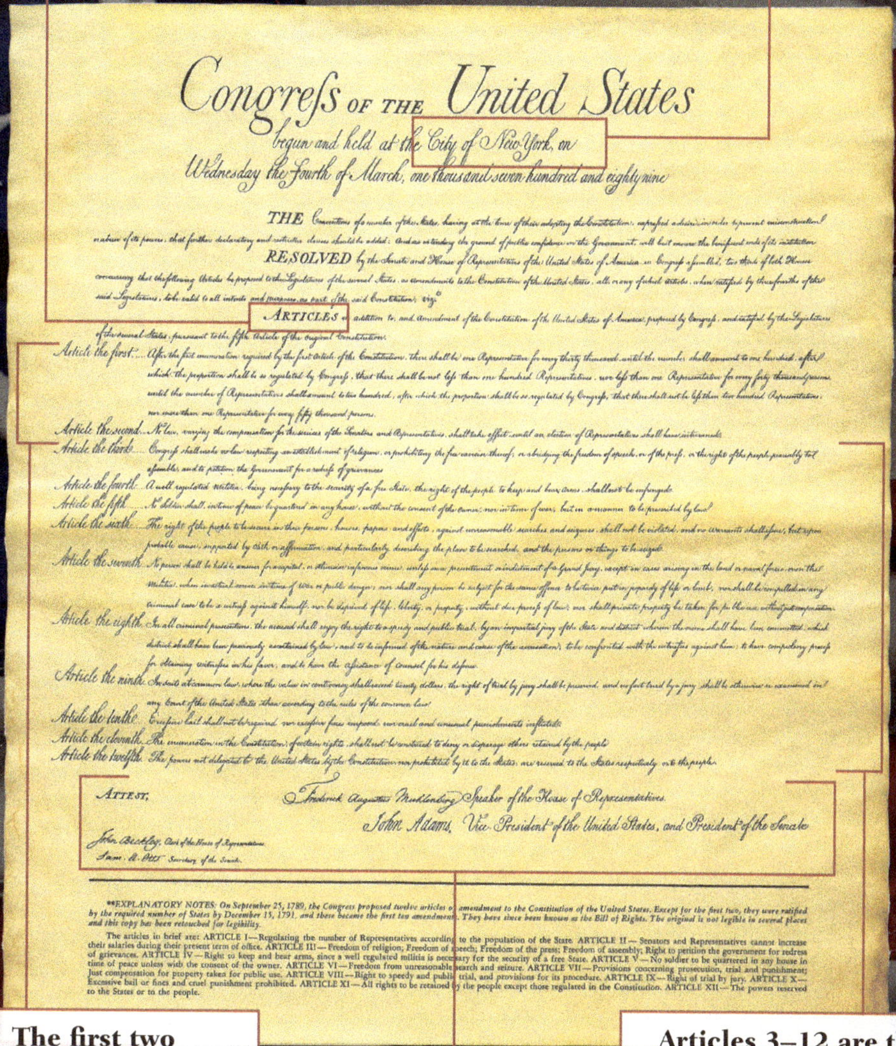
Congress of the United States
begun and held at the City of New-York, on
Wednesday the fourth of March, one thousand seven hundred and eighty nine

Attest,

Frederick Augustus Muhlenberg Speaker of the House of Representatives.
John Adams, Vice-President of the United States, and President of the Senate

John Beckley, Clerk of the House of Representatives.
Sam. A. Otis Secretary of the Senate.

**EXPLANATORY NOTES: On September 25, 1789, the Congress proposed twelve articles of amendment to the Constitution of the United States. Except for the first two, they were ratified by the required number of States by December 15, 1791, and these became the first ten amendments. They have since been known as the Bill of Rights. The original is not legible in several places and this copy has been retouched for legibility.

The articles in brief are: ARTICLE I—Regulating the number of Representatives according to the population of the State. ARTICLE II—Senators and Representatives cannot increase their salaries during their present term of office. ARTICLE III—Freedom of religion; Freedom of speech; Freedom of the press; Freedom of assembly; Right to petition the government for redress of grievances. ARTICLE IV—Right to keep and bear arms, since a well regulated militia is necessary for the security of a free State. ARTICLE V—No soldier to be quartered in any house in time of peace unless with the consent of the owner. ARTICLE VI—Freedom from unreasonable search and seizure. ARTICLE VII—Provisions concerning prosecution, trial and punishment; Just compensation for property taken for public use. ARTICLE VIII—Right to speedy and public trial, and provisions for its procedure. ARTICLE IX—Right of trial by jury. ARTICLE X—Excessive bail or fines and cruel punishment prohibited. ARTICLE XI—All rights to be retained by the people except those regulated in the Constitution. ARTICLE XII—The powers reserved to the States or to the people.

The first two amendments weren't ratified by the states.

Articles 3–12 are the Bill of Rights as we know it today.

Signed by:
Frederick Augustus Muhlenberg - Speaker of the House
John Adams - Vice President
John Beckley - Clerk of the House of Representatives
Sam A. Otis - Secretary of the Senate

OTHER AMENDMENTS

The Bill of Rights is made up of the first 10 amendments to the U.S. Constitution. As of 2016, 17 amendments have followed it. These amendments—like those in the Bill of Rights—were drafted because Americans felt the Constitution needed to be changed to reflect the needs of U.S. citizens at a particular time in American history.

Certain amendments focus on protecting and granting individual rights to different groups of Americans. The 14th Amendment states all people born or **naturalized** in America—including those who'd once been slaves—are citizens of the United States. This means the Bill of Rights applies to them, too. The 15th Amendment protects citizens' right to vote no matter their race, and the 19th Amendment gives women the right to vote.

This chart shows the 17 amendments to the U.S. Constitution that were ratified after the Bill of Rights.

Amendments After the Bill of Rights

11th (1795)	*protects states from lawsuits brought by citizens of other states or countries*
12th (1804)	*changes the presidential election process*
13th (1865)	*ends slavery*
14th (1868)	*grants African Americans citizenship and equal rights*
15th (1870)	*states that all men—regardless of race—have the right to vote*
16th (1913)	*creates a federal income tax*
17th (1913)	*allows for the direct election of U.S. senators*
18th (1919)	*outlaws the making and sale of alcohol*
19th (1920)	*gives women the right to vote*
20th (1933)	*changes the dates for the start and end of terms for presidents and members of Congress*
21st (1933)	***repeals** the 18th Amendment*
22nd (1951)	*limits presidents to serving two terms*
23rd (1961)	*gives citizens of Washington, D.C., the right to choose **electors** in presidential elections*
24th (1964)	*makes it illegal to tax people before they can vote for president*
25th (1967)	*sets up the official order for who becomes president and vice president if the offices are **vacated***
26th (1971)	*lowers the voting age to 18*
27th (1992)	*makes it so Congress members' pay can't be changed until after an election*

REFLECTING A CHANGING AMERICA

The Bill of Rights is as important now as it was when it was ratified more than 200 years ago. Americans' lives have changed a lot since 1791, but one thing that hasn't changed is the belief that individual rights matter. The protection of these rights is an essential part of a strong democratic government, so the Bill of Rights continues to be considered one of the foundations of U.S. democracy.

Today, the Bill of Rights is at the center of many debates about individual rights in a changing America. Discussions about gun control, free speech, religious freedom, states' rights, and police searches all have their roots in the Bill of Rights. Even though this document was written long ago, it still has the power to affect the lives of all U.S. citizens.

GLOSSARY

diversity: The state of having many different forms or types.

draft: To put into written form.

elector: A member of the electoral college, which is the group of representatives that elects the president and vice president of the United States.

ensure: To make certain.

incriminate: To show proof of involvement in a crime.

naturalize: To make a person a citizen.

persecution: Cruel treatment, especially because of a person's race or religious or political beliefs.

petition: To make a request.

procedure: A series of steps followed in a set order.

repeal: To do away with.

riot: A violent public disturbance by a group of people.

vacate: To leave something empty.

warrant: A document issued by a legal or government official giving a law enforcement officer permission to take action to carry out the law.

INDEX

WEBSITES

Due to the changing nature of Internet links, PowerKids Press has developed an online list of websites related to the subject of this book. This site is updated regularly. Please use this link to access the list: www.powerkidslinks.com/amdoc/bor